ENGLISH TIME

WORKBOOK 1

Melanie Graham
Stanton Procter

OXFORD
UNIVERSITY PRESS

OXFORD
UNIVERSITY PRESS

198 Madison Avenue
New York, NY 10016 USA

Great Clarendon Street
Oxford OX2 6DP England

Oxford New York

Auckland Cape Town Dar es Salaam Hong Kong Karachi
Kuala Lumpur Madrid Melbourne Mexico City Nairobi
New Delhi Shanghai Taipei Toronto

With offices in

Argentina Austria Brazil Chile Czech Republic France Greece
Guatemala Hungary Italy Japan South Korea Poland Portugal
Singapore Switzerland Thailand Turkey Ukraine Vietnam

OXFORD is a trademark of Oxford University Press.

ISBN : 978 0 19 436307 5

Editorial Manager: Shelagh Speers
Senior Editor: Lesley Koustaff
Editor: Genevieve Kocienda
Senior Production Editor: Joseph McGasko
Elementary Design Manager: Doris Chen Pinzon
Designer: Lana Cheng
Art Buyer: Laura Nash
Production Manager: Shanta Persaud
Production Assistant: Zainaltu Jawat Ali

Illustrators: Yvette Banek, Shirley Beckes/Craven Design, Terri
and Joe Chicko, Anne Iosa, Stephanie Peterson,
Zina Saunders, Susan Simon, Jim Talbot

Original characters developed by Amy Wummer
Cover illustration: Cheryl Mendenhall
Additional cover art: Jim Talbot
Cover design: Silver Editions

Printing (last digit): 20 19 18 17 16 15 14 13 12 11

Printed in Hong Kong.

The Alphabet

Trace and write.

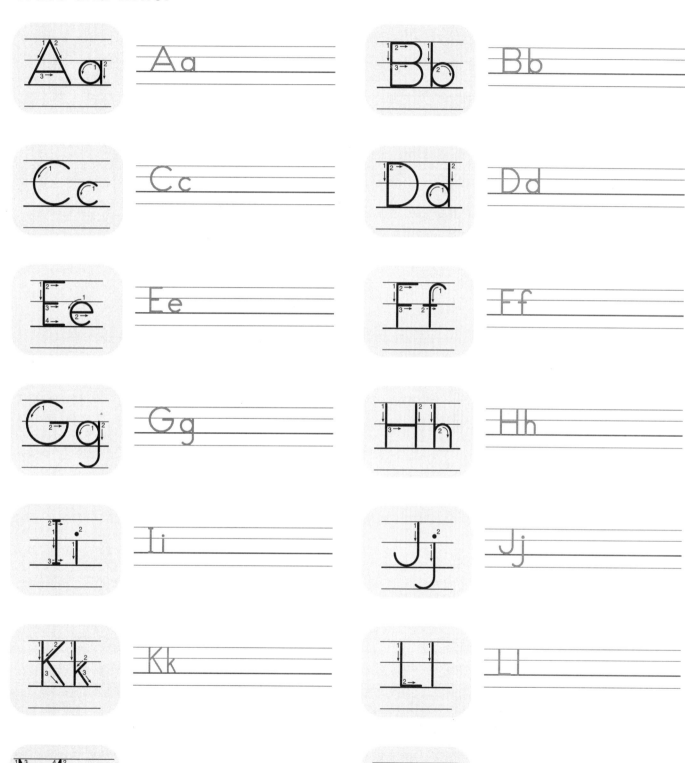

Conversation Time

Good morning.

Hello! How are you?

Fine, thank you.

A. Read and match.

1. Good morning.

2. Hello! How are you?

3. Fine, thank you.

B. Look and write.

Hello   are   morning   thank

1. Good _____.

2. _____ ! How _____ you?

3. Fine, _____ you.

Annie   Ted   Digger   girl   boy   dog

A. Look and match.

1.    2.    3.    4.    5.    6.

Annie   Ted   Digger

girl   boy   dog

B. Write the letter.

1. ___b___ Annie

2. _____ Ted

3. _____ Digger

4. _____ boy

5. _____ girl

6. _____ dog

Practice Time

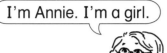

I'm Annie. I'm a girl.

You're Ted. You're a boy.

A. Look and match.

1.
2.
3.
4.
5.
6.

I'm Digger. I'm a dog.

You're Annie. You're a girl.

You're Ted. You're a boy.

I'm Ted. I'm a boy.

You're Digger. You're a dog.

I'm Annie. I'm a girl.

B. Your turn. Draw and write.

I'm _____

I'm a _____

Phonics Time

ball   pencil   boy   pizza   bird   pig

A. Does it begin with b or p? Look and circle.

1. b / p

2. b p

3.  b p

4.  b p

5.  b p

6. b p

7. b p

8. b p

B. Match and say.

1.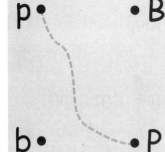
   p •   • B
   b •   • P

2.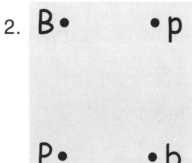
   B •   • p
   P •   • b

3.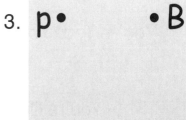
   p •   • B
   b •   • P

C. Look and write.

1.
   izza

2.
   encil

3.
   ird

Ah-choo!

Bless you!

Thanks.

A. Read and match.

1. Ah-choo!

2. Bless you!

3. Thanks.

B. Unscramble, match, and write.

1. lsseb ouy •   • Ah-choo!

2. kahtns •   • Bless you!   Bless you!

3. ha-ocoh •   • Thanks.

| butterfly | tree | bird | lake | flower | cloud |

A. Look and circle.

1.  lake
cloud

2.  tree
flower

3.  bird
butterfly

4.  flower
cloud

5.  flower
lake

6.  bird
tree

B. Look and write.

1.  _____

2.  _____

3.  _____

4.  _____

5. _____

6. _____

This is a butterfly.

That's a bird.

A. Look and circle.

1.   this
      that

2.   this
      that

3.   this
      that

4.   this
      that

B. Look and write.

1. _____ is a _____

2. _____

3. _____

4. _____

C. Your turn. Draw and write.

This _____

That's _____

Phonics Time

kite

girl

kangaroo

key

gorilla

garden

A. Does it begin with g or k? Circle and write.

1. 　g
　　　(k)

key

2. 　g
　　　k

3. 　g
　　　k

B. Which pictures begin with the same sound? Circle.

1.

2.

3.

4.

C. Match and say.

1.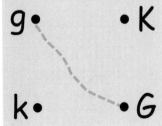

g •　　• K

k •　　• G

2.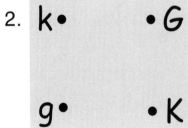

k •　　• G

g •　　• K

3.

G •　　• g

K •　　• k

A. Read and match.

1. Sh! Be quiet!

2. Sorry.

3. That's okay.

B. Look and write.

okay   quiet   Sorry   .

1. Sh! Be _____

2. _____

3. That's _____

Word Time

| sheep | horse | cow | chicken | pig | cat |

A. Look and match.

1.    2.   3.    4.   5.   6.

sheep   horse   pig   cat   chicken   cow

B. Find and circle.

horhorseckpicattgmslapigchsheepfambccowchickenrhose

C. Unscramble and write.

1. h p s e e _____ sheep _____   2. t a c _____

3. g p i _____   4. e h r o s _____

5. h e c k c i n _____   6. o w c _____

A. Look and write.

1.    What's _____ ?   It's _____

2.

3.

4.

5.

6.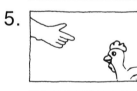

B. Your turn. Draw and write.

What's _____ ?

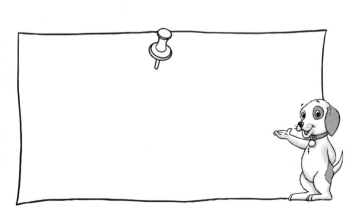

Phonics Time

nurse

mother

net

milk

mop

night

A. Which picture begins with the letter? Write ✓.

1. m
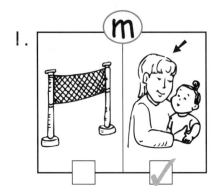
☐ ✓

2. n

☐ ☐

3. m
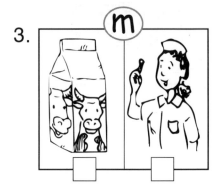
☐ ☐

4. n
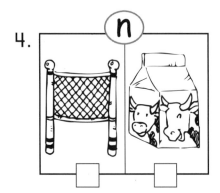
☐ ☐

5. n
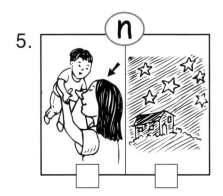
☐ ☐

6. m
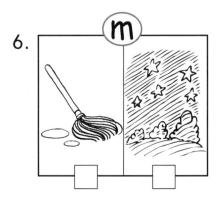
☐ ☐

B. Which pictures begin with the letter? Circle.

m

n
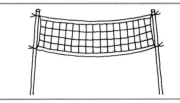

A. Look and match.

1.
2.
3.
4.
5.
6.

You're a dog.

That's a horse.

This is a butterfly.

I'm Ted.

What's that?
It's a bird.

I'm a girl.

B. Look and circle.

1.

won   sow   cow

2.

cat   tac   cab

3.

bred   bird   drab

4.

kale   leak   lake

5.

girl   hurl   grill

6.

tee   tree   three

A. Look at the numbers. Write the sentence.

1	a	2	I'm	3	is	4	you	5	You're
6	Annie	7	morning	8	This	9	are	10	Thanks.
11	Good	12	tree	13	girl	14	boy	15	How
16	That's	17	flower	18	?	19	.	20	Ted

1. | 11 | 7 | 19 | 15 | 9 | 4 | 18 |

   Good

2. | 2 | 6 | 19 | 2 | 1 | 13 | 19 |

3. | 5 | 20 | 19 | 5 | 1 | 14 | 19 |

4. | 8 | 3 | 1 | 17 | 19 | 16 | 1 | 12 | 19 |

B. Which picture begins with a different sound? Write X.

1.

2.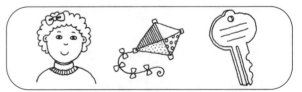

3.

4.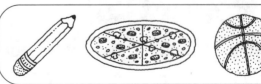

Here you are. Thanks. You're welcome.

A. Look and write.

Thanks   welcome   you   .

1. Here _____ are.

2. _____

3. You're _____

B. Unscramble, match, and write.

1. oyu're celwemo •   • Here you are.   _____

2. eehr oyu rea •   • Thanks.   _____

3. haktns •   • You're welcome.   _____

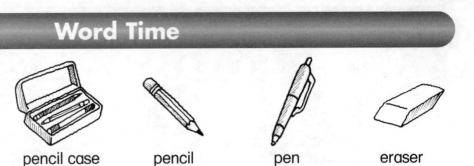

ruler   book   pencil case   pencil   pen   eraser

A. Write the letter.

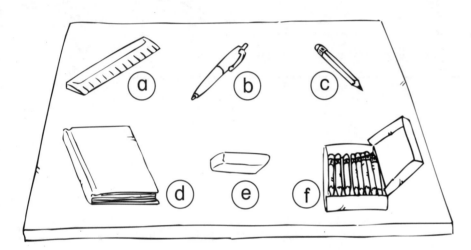

1. ____d____ book

2. _____ eraser

3. _____ pen

4. _____ pencil

5. _____ pencil case

6. _____ ruler

B. Read the question. Write the answer.

1. What's this?

It's a

2. What's this?

3. What's this?

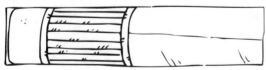

4. What's this?

Practice Time

Is it a pen?
Yes, it is.

Is it an eraser?
No, it isn't. It's a ruler.

A. Look and circle.

1. 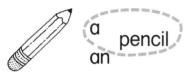 a (pencil) / an

2. a / an pen

3. a / an eraser

4. a / an pencil case

5. a / an ruler

6. a / an book

B. Read the question. Write the answer.

1. Is it a book?

_____

2. Is it a ruler?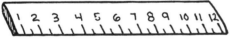

_____

3. Is it an eraser?

_____

4. Is it a pencil?

_____

dog   tiger   desk   teacher   duck   table

A. Does it begin with d or t? Write the word.

d words   desk

t words

B. What letter does it begin with? Read and write ✓.

d										
t	✓									
b										
p										
g										
k										
m										
n										

 What's your first name? Annie. What's your last name?  Day.

A. Look and write.

last   Lee   name   ?   Ted   What's   .   your

1.

What's your first name? _____

2. _____

B. Look and circle.

Tommy Lin

1. What's your first / last name?    Tommy.

2. What's your first / last name?    Lin.

C. Your turn. Read the question. Write the answer.

What's your first name? _____

What's your last name? _____

Word Time

1	one	2	two	3	three
4	four	5	five	6	six
7	seven	8	eight	9	nine
10	ten	11	eleven	12	twelve

A. Write the number.

1. one ___1___   2. four _____   3. eleven _____   4. six _____

B. Write the word.

1. 12 _twelve_   2. 8 _____   3. 2 _____

4. 7 _____   5. 3 _____   6. 10 _____

C. Look and match.

1.   2.   3.    4. 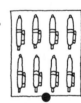   5.    6.

two trees   one boy   five cows

eight pens   four dogs   twelve birds

D. Find and circle the numbers.

twetwelvethoneveininehtelevenonfourixsevenen

Practice Time

A. Count and write.

1.  six pigs

2.  _____

3.  _____

4.  _____

B. Look and write.

1. How many books?

_____

2. _____

_____

3. _____

_____

4. _____

_____

Phonics Time

water

hand

woman

house
window
horse

A. Does it begin with h or w? Look and match.

1.
2.
3.
4.
5.
6.

ẇ   ḣ

B. Match and say.

1. h• •H
   w• •W

2. W• •h
   H• •w

3. h• •W
   w• •H

C. Does it begin with h or w? Circle and write.

1. h
   w
   _____

2.  h
   w
   _____

3. h
   w
   _____

4. h
   w
   _____

5. h
   w
   _____

6. h
   w
   _____

A. Read and match.

1. Ouch!

2. Are you okay?

3. I think so.

B. Unscramble and match.

1. ear oyu kaoy •

2. i hkint os •

3. chou •

• Ouch!

• Are you okay?

• I think so.

C. Circle and write.

1. !ouch
   Ouch!
   ouch!

2. are you okay?
   ?are you okay
   Are you okay?

3. !I think so
   I think so.
   i think so.

Word Time

| happy | sad | hot | cold | hungry | thirsty |

A. Look and write.

1.

2.

3.

4.

5.

6.

B. Read and complete the pictures.

I'm cold.

I'm happy.

I'm sad.

I'm hot.

C. Your turn. Draw and write.

I'm

Practice Time

 Are you happy?

 Yes, I am.

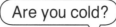 Are you cold?

 No, I'm not. I'm hot.

A. Look and write.

1.  _____ hungry?

2.  _____ cold?

3.  _____ happy?

4. _____ thirsty?

B. Your turn. Read the question. Write the answer.

1. Are you happy? _____

2. Are you sad? _____

Phonics Time

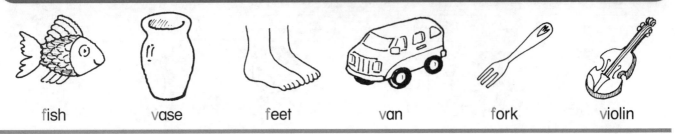

fish   vase   feet   van   fork   violin

A. Which pictures begin with the letter? Circle.

B. Look and write.

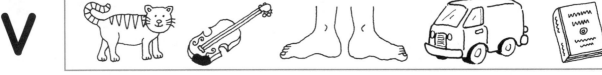

1.   2.   3.

4.   5.   6.

C. Match and say.

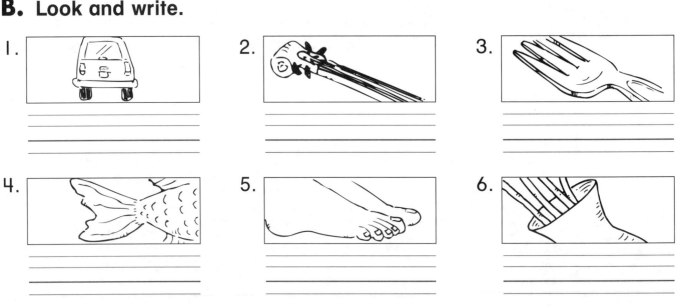

d   n   k   p   b   w   f   t   g   m   v   h

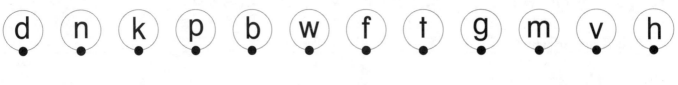

G   M   T   F   P   N   D   K   V   W   H   B

A. Look and match.

1. • • Sh! Be quiet!

2. • • Good morning.

3. • • Here you are!

4. • • What's your first name? Annie.

5. • • Ouch!

B. Write the letter.

1. _____ book

2. _____ happy

3. _____ flower

4. _____ hot

5. _____ pencil

6. _____ ruler

Review 2

A. Read and circle the mistakes.

1.

good morning?
my name is ted.
what's your first name.

2.

this is a butterfly.
what's that!
is it a cloud.

3.

hello.
how are you.
are you hungry.

4.

this is an eraser?
is it a pen.
no! it isn't. it's a pencil!

B. Complete the puzzle.

ACROSS ➡

1.

2.

3.

4.

5.

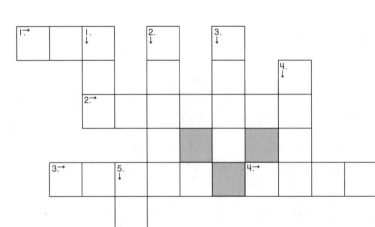
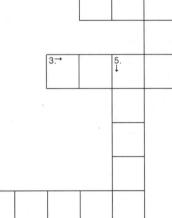

DOWN ⬇

1.

2.

3.

4.

5.

 Are you finished?    No, not yet.   Please hurry!

A. Circle and write.

1. Are _____ finished?

 you   Ted   I

2. No, _____ yet.

 net   not   night

3. Please _____!

 happy   house   hurry

B. Read and connect.

1. Are   hurry   finished   ?

2. No,   you   yet

3. Please   not   !   •

Word Time

| pizza | hamburgers | sushi | noodles | dumplings | fried rice |

A. Look and match.

1.  2.   3.   4.  5.   6.

noodles   fried rice   sushi   dumplings   hamburgers   pizza

   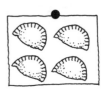 

B. Unscramble and write.

1. huiss

2. minpludsg

3. dolsone

4. zazip

5. mebgarshur

6. dreif crie

C. Find and circle.

pizzalingsnoodlesushdumplingsershamburgersapfriedric emilsushi

Practice Time

I like noodles.
You like noodles.
I don't like hamburgers.
You don't like hamburgers.

A. Read and write ✓ or ✗.

☐ 1. I don't like noodles.

☐ 2. I like sushi.

☐ 3. I like hamburgers.

☐ 4. I like pizza.

☐ 5. I don't like fried rice.

☐ 6. I don't like dumplings.

B. Unscramble and write.

1.    don't / . / you / noodles / like

    You _____

2.   pizza / like / . / you

C. Your turn. Draw and write.

Phonics Time

soup

zebra

sea

zipper

sock

zoo

A. Does it begin with s or z? Circle and write.

1.   S   Z

2.    S   Z

3.    S   Z

B. Which picture begins with a different sound? Write X.

1.

2.

3.

4.

C. Which pictures begin with the letter? Circle.

S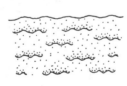

Z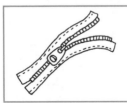

May I borrow a pen?

Sure. Here you are.

Thanks.

A. Look and write.

are   borrow   Here   you   I   pencil   a   Thanks   May   .

1. May _____ ?

2. Sure. _____

3. _____

B. Circle and write.

1. May I borrow a _____ ?

   pig   pen   ten

2. _____ . Here you are.

   Soup   Sea   Sure

3. _____

   Thanks   Three   Thirsty

Word Time

 bananas   oranges  potatoes  apples  cucumbers  carrots

A. Count and write.

1. three apples

2.

3.

4.

5.

6.

B. Unscramble and write.

1. p e a l p s

2. o o t p a s e t

3. a b n a s a n

4. r t a c r s o

5. e g a r n o s

6. r s u u m c e c b

Practice Time

Do you like apples?

Yes, I do.

Do you like potatoes?

No, I don't.

A. Look and write.

1.
_____ carrots?
_____
_____
_____

2.
_____
_____
_____
_____

3.
_____
_____
_____
_____

4.
_____
_____
_____
_____

B. Your turn. Read the question. Write the answer.

1. Do you like carrots? _____
_____

2. Do you like apples? _____
_____

bag

ant

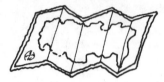
map

hat

A. Circle and write.

1. bag
tag

_____

2.  map
nap

_____

3.  hat
bat

_____

4. ant
add

_____

B. Circle the short a words.

1. cow
pig
cat

2. sad
hot
cold

3. dog
bat
bird

4. mop
pen
pan

5. top
map
bed

C. Does it have short a? Circle.

Unit 8

 What's wrong?  I feel sick.  That's too bad.

A. Circle and write.

1. What's _____?

   water   wrong   window

2. I feel _____.

   sock   soup   sick

3. That's too _____.

   bag   bad   bat

B. Unscramble, match, and write.

1. i efle kics •   • What's wrong? _____

2. s'hatt oto bda •   • I feel sick. _____

3. t'sawh grown •   • That's too bad. _____

Word Time

  tall
 short
 fat
 thin
 young
 old

A. Circle and write.

1.   young / old

_____

2.   short / tall

_____

3.   short / fat

_____

4.   thin / fat

_____

5.   tall / short

_____

6.  old / young

_____

B. Write the letter.

1. _____ a fat cat

2. _____ an old pig

3. _____ a short girl

4. _____ a tall boy

5. _____ a young dog

6. _____ a thin cow

Practice Time

 She's young. She isn't old.

 He's thin. He isn't fat.

A. Look and match.

1.
2.
3.
4.
5.
6.

He's fat. He isn't thin.

She's old. She isn't young.

She's short. She isn't tall.

He's young. He isn't old.

She's thin. She isn't fat.

He's tall. He isn't short.

B. Look and write.

1.

2.

3.

egg   pen   bed   vet

A. Look and write.

1.   2.   3.

4.   5.   6.

1. p e n

B. Which pictures have the vowel sound? Circle.

short **e**

short **a**

C. Circle the words you can read.

How many words can you read? _____

egg pen pan hat mad beg net Sam pen get fed bat men pet dad van hem

A. Read and connect.

1. May I borrow a pen? •   • No, not yet. •   • That's too bad.

2. What's wrong? •   • Sure. Here you are. •   • Thanks.

3. Are you finished? •   • I feel sick. •   • Please hurry!

4. Ouch! •   • Thanks. •   • I think so.

5. Here you are. •   • Are you okay? •   • You're welcome.

B. Look and write.

1. _____   2. _____   3. _____

4. _____   5. _____   6. _____

7. _____   8. _____   9. _____

10. _____   11. _____   12. _____

A. Read and circle the mistakes.

1.
what's that.
it's pizza?
i don't like pizza?

2.
i like apples!
do you like apples.
yes, i do?

3.
i'm annie.
i'm a girl?
i'm young?

4.
this is ted?
he's young.
he isn't old?

B. Read and match.

1. three tall trees　　2. two short boys　　3. two old dogs　　4. one fat pig

C. Look and match.

1. 　2. 　3. 　4.

I like apples.

He's tall. He isn't short.

You don't like oranges.

He's hungry. He isn't thirsty.

What's your telephone number?

It's 765-1234.

Pardon me?   765-1234.

A. Read the question. Write the answer.

612-4321

761-3942

881-9841

235-6011

What's your telephone number?

1. _____

2. _____

3. _____

4. _____

B. Read and circle.

| 1. What's | you
yellow
your | telephone | name?
number?
nurse? |

2. It's 769-1485.

| 3. | Pencil
Please
Pardon | me? |

4. 769-1485.

C. Your turn. Read the question. Write the answer.

What's your telephone number? _____

Word Time

 police officer

 nurse

 mail carrier

 teacher

 firefighter

 doctor

A. Which picture is different? Circle and write.

1.
_____

2.
_____

3.
_____

4.
_____

5.
_____

B. Look and write.

1. He's a _____ .

2.  _____

3.  _____

4.  _____

Is he a doctor? Yes, he is.

Is she a teacher? No, she isn't. She's a firefighter.

A. Read the question. Write the answer.

1. Is he a teacher?

2. Is she a firefighter?

3. Is he a mail carrier?

4. Is she a doctor?

B. Look and write.

1.

   nurse?

   No,

2.

   police officer?

Phonics Time

dig

sit

pin

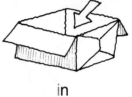
in

A. Look and write.

i	s	p	n	d	g	c	k	t

1. ■★■

pig

2. ★◆
_____

3. ●★✚
_____

4. ●★◆▲
_____

5. ●★■
_____

6. ■★◆
_____

7. ▲★✚
_____

8. ✚★◆
_____

B. Circle the short i words.

1.
pen
pin
pan

2.
in
on
an

3.
Sam
set
sip

4.
pig
peg
pat

5.
is
sad
sit

C. Does it have short i? Write ✓ or ✗.

1. ☐

2. ☐

3.  ☐

4.  ☐

5. ☐

6. ☐

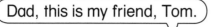
Dad, this is my friend, Tom.

Nice to meet you, Tom.   Hello.

A. Look and write.

| friend | Hello | Nice | this | . | you |

1. Dad, _____ is my _____, Sam.

2. _____ to meet _____, Sam.

3. _____

B. Unscramble and write.

1. my / , / Pam / Mom / . / is / , / this / friend

   Mom, this is _____

2. Pam / . / you / meet / , / to / Nice

   _____

3. . / Hello

   _____

Word Time

 draw a picture

 play basketball

 drive a car

 ride a bike

 climb a tree

 sing a song

A. Look and circle.

1.
drive
ride a bike

2.
sing
play a song

3.
climb
play basketball

4.
drive
sing a car

5.
play
climb a tree

6.
drive
draw a picture

B. Complete the puzzle.

1. 2. 3. 4. 5. 6.

1. r i d e a b i k e

What is the mystery word? _____

Unit 11

Practice Time

A. Look and circle.

1.

She	can	draw a picture.
He	can't	ride a bike.
		sing a song.

2.

I	can	drive a car.
You	can't	ride a bike.
It		climb a tree.

3.

I	can	draw a picture.
You	can't	climb a tree.
It		play basketball.

B. Look and write.

1.

You _____ .

2.

He _____ .

3.

It _____ .

Phonics Time

on

mop

hot

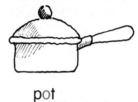
pot

A. Look and write.

1.
2.
3.
4.
5.
6.

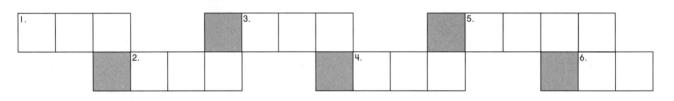

B. Circle the short o words.

1.	2.	3.	4.	5.
hit	pig	fig	pot	dad
hot	dot	map	pat	mop
hat	bed	Tom	pit	pin

C. Which pictures have the vowel sound? Circle.

short **a**

short **e**

short **i**

short **o**
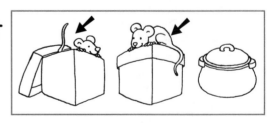

 I'm going now.

 Bye-bye!

 See you tomorrow.

A. Read and match.

1. I'm going now.

2. Bye-bye!

3. See you tomorrow.

B. Circle and write.

1. i'm going now.

   I'm going now.

   I'm going now?

2. Bye-bye!

   bye-bye?

   !bye-bye

3. see you tomorrow.

   ?See you tomorrow

   See you tomorrow.

fly
a kite

use
chopsticks

make
a sandwich

swim

play
the guitar

do
a cartwheel

A. Circle and write.

1.

make
fly
a sandwich

_____

2.

do
play
the guitar

_____

3.

use
do
a cartwheel

_____

4.

play
fly
a kite

_____

B. Unscramble and write.

1. od a rlecwetha

_____

2. kema a chasdiwn

_____

3. eus spictkchos

_____

4. lyf a tiek

_____

5. miws

_____

6. lyap het ritagu

_____

A. Read the question. Check (✓) the correct answer.

1. Can she do a cartwheel?

☐ Yes, she can.

☐ No, she can't.

2. Can he play the guitar?

☐ Yes, he can.

☐ No, he can't.

3. Can it swim?

☐ Yes, it can.

☐ No, it can't.

4. Can he use chopsticks?

☐ Yes, he can.

☐ No, he can't.

B. Look and write.

1.

Can she _____ ?

Yes, _____

2.

3.

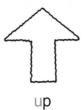
up

bus

nut

sun

A. Find and circle.

s	a	n	e	t
u	b	u	s	a
v	e	s	u	n
z	n	u	p	o
n	u	t	a	t

B. Circle the short u words and pictures.

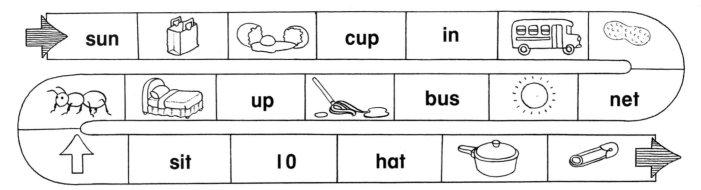

C. Does it have short u? Circle and write.

1.  _____

2. 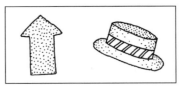 _____

3. 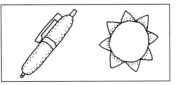 _____

4. 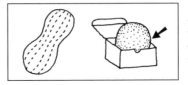 _____

54

Unit 12

A. Circle the mistakes. Then rewrite the sentences.

1. (see) You tomorrow(?)

   See you tomorrow.

2. dad. this is My friend! kim.

3. what's your Telephone number.

B. Look and write.

1.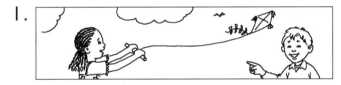

   _____ can _____ .

2.

   _____ She's _____ .

3.

   _____ can _____ .

4.

C. Read and match.

1. Can she drive a car?
    No, she can't.

2. You can't swim.

3. Is she a doctor?
    Yes, she is.

4. I can swim.

A. Look and write.

1.
_____
_____

2.
_____
_____

3.
_____
_____

4.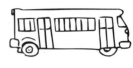
_____
_____

5.
_____
_____

6.
_____
_____

7.
_____
_____

8.
_____
_____

B. Read the question. Write the answer.

1.  Can she fly a kite?
_____
_____
_____

2. Is she a mail carrier?
_____
_____
_____

3.  Can she swim?
_____
_____
_____

C. Your turn. Draw and write what you can do.

I can _____

A. Read and connect.

1. Ah-choo! •   • Thanks. •   • That's okay.

2. Good morning. •   • No, not yet. •   • Thank you.

3. Here you are. •   • Hello! How are you? • • You're welcome.

4. Sh! Be quiet! •   • Bless you! •   • Fine, thank you.

5. Are you finished? •   • Sorry. •   • Please hurry!

B. Read and connect.

1. What's wrong? •   • Nice to meet you, Sue. • • I think so.

2. Ouch! •   • Bye-bye. •   • Thanks.

3. May I borrow a pen? • • Are you okay? •   • That's too bad.

4. I'm going now. •   • I feel sick. •   • Hello.

5. Dad, this is my friend, Sue. • • Sure. Here you are. • • See you tomorrow.

A. Complete the puzzle.

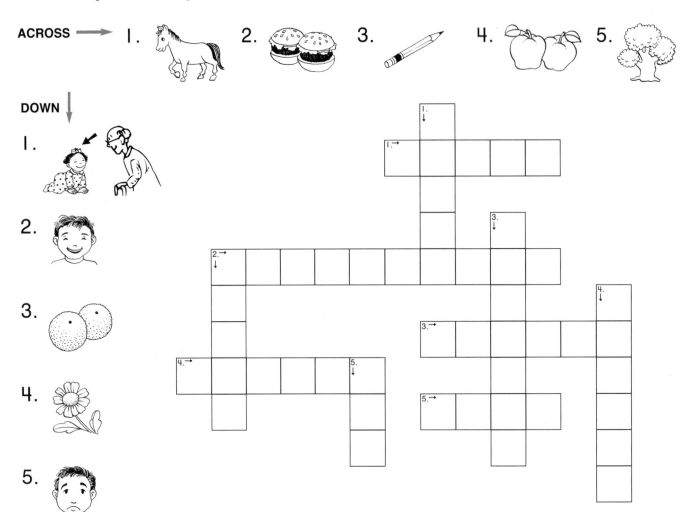

ACROSS ➡
1.
2.
3.
4.
5.

DOWN ⬇
1.
2.
3.
4.
5.

B. Which picture is different? Write ✗.

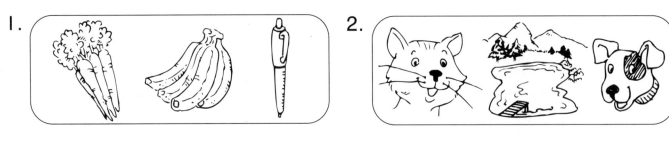

1.
2.

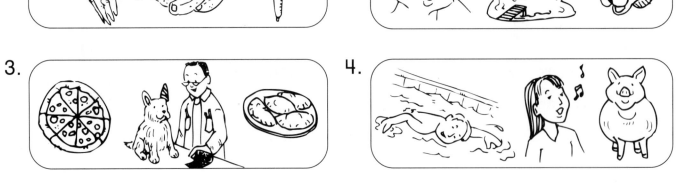

3.
4.

A. Read and match.

1. What's that? •   • Twelve books.

2. I'm Annie. I'm a girl. •   • She can ride a bike.

3. Is it a pen? •   • It's a horse.

4. He can swim. •   • Yes, I am.

5. How many books? •   • You're Ted. You're a boy.

6. Are you happy? •   • No, it isn't. It's a pencil.

B. Read and match.

1. Do you like bananas? •   • She isn't tall.

2. This is a lake. •   • You don't like hamburgers.

3. Is he a teacher? •   • Yes, he can.

4. I like pizza. •   • No, I don't.

5. Can he swim? •   • No, he isn't. He's a doctor.

6. She's short. •   • That's a tree.

Phonics Time Review

A. Circle the words you can read.

How many words can you read? _____

cat hat ant pen bed vet in sit dig hot pot on mop sun nut bus up

B. Which picture begins with a different sound? Write ✗.

1.

2.
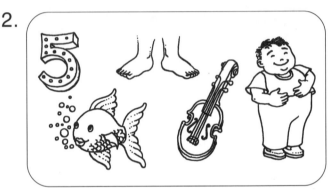

3.

4.

C. Match and say.

a i t m g u e w o v n z s h

T G V O Z A H M S W U N I E